£8.99

629.2

15285L

INSIDE A
CAR

MIKE FLYNN

angus

This edition published in 2004
by Angus Books Ltd
12 Ravensbury Terrace
London SW18 4RL

ISBN 1-904594-48-4

FOR BROWN PARTWORKS
Project editor: Roland Hall
Consultant: Dr. Derek Smith
Designer: Sarah Williams
Illustrator: Matthew White (main artwork), Mark Walker
Managing editor: Anne O'Daly
Picture researcher: Sean Hannaway

Production by Omnipress,
Eastbourne, UK
Printed and bound in Dubai

Contents

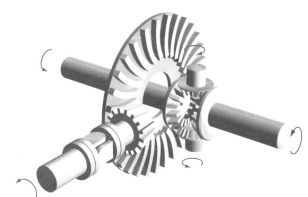

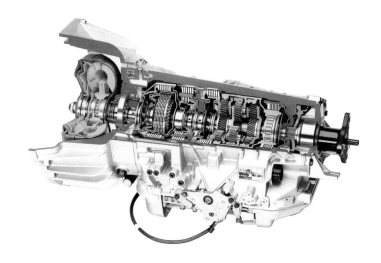

How it all started

The car as we know it began life as a very different machine. The first car was powered by steam and used to pull guns across fields. Many types of road vehicle have been invented, but all modern cars are based on a design first built over 100 years ago.

Karl Benz at the wheel of an early car in 1887. It was called a "Patent–Motor–Wagen."

In 1769 a French engineer called Nicolas-Joseph Cugnot (1725–1804) designed a steam engine that was small but powerful enough to drive a three-wheeled gun carriage across land. Several years later British inventor Richard Trevithick (1771–1833) built his first working steam-driven carriage in 1801. In 1803 he caused a stir by driving his second steam-driven carriage around the streets of London. Unfortunately, steam-powered cars did not have a future. Steam engines are too heavy, dirty, and inefficient. If there was to be any real improvement, another way had to be found to power road vehicles.

Above: This magazine shows the start of the first automobile race. It was held in France in 1895.

Internal combustion

Before the century was over, a couple of German engineers—Gottlieb Daimler (1834–1900) and Karl Benz (1844–1929)—revolutionized automobile design with the introduction of the petrol-powered internal combustion engine. Smaller, lighter, and more powerful than the steam engine, the internal combustion engine from around 1880 made possible the idea of the automobile as we know it. This was reflected in Daimler's new car of 1889, which had an internal combustion engine fitted at the rear, four gears, and belt-driven wheels. It was made from a lightweight tubular steel frame.

Dramatic changes

The first real car race took place shortly after the introduction of the internal combustion engine. It was held in 1895 in France and ran from Paris to Bordeaux and back, a distance of 732 miles (1,178km). At this time cars were expensive because they were custom

FACT FILE

⦿ **Most automobile manufacturers have their own web sites. Here are some examples for you to look at:**
http://www.ford.com
http://www.gm.com
http://www.mercedes.com
http://www.ferrari.it

A production line in the United States in 1914. The engine has been attached to the chassis. The body panels have yet to be added.

built (you had to order one to be built specially for you). This changed in 1908 when Henry Ford (1863–1947) introduced the Model T in the United States. The Model T was produced using modern factory production-line methods. It proved so popular that by 1927 there were 15 million Model Ts on the road. Using similar techniques, the

Germans developed the Volkswagen Beetle in 1937. It was a mass-produced, low-priced car that proved to be very popular all over the world. Over in England, in 1959, Sir Alec Issigonis (1906—1988) developed the Mini. Tiny, cheap, and yet able to carry four adults, the Mini proved to be a winner from the start and is still on sale.

This is the one-millionth Beetle to be built. Beetles are still driven all around the world.

Inside a car

The car is a complex machine made up of around 14,000 different parts. The body is usually made from moulded steel. The body and the chassis are integral (all joined together) and support the engine, axles, transmission, gas tank, suspension, steering, and brakes.

Airbag
This is an important safety device that you can't even see.

Engine
This is where the power to drive the car comes from. You put in the fuel, create a spark, and the pistons start moving. This makes the driveshaft move.

Suspension
Springs and shock absorbers are essential to give a smooth ride when the car goes over bumps or holes in the road. Each wheel has its own separate suspension.

Brakes
The footbrake acts on all four wheels and is controlled by the driver's feet. The handbrake acts on the rear wheels only.

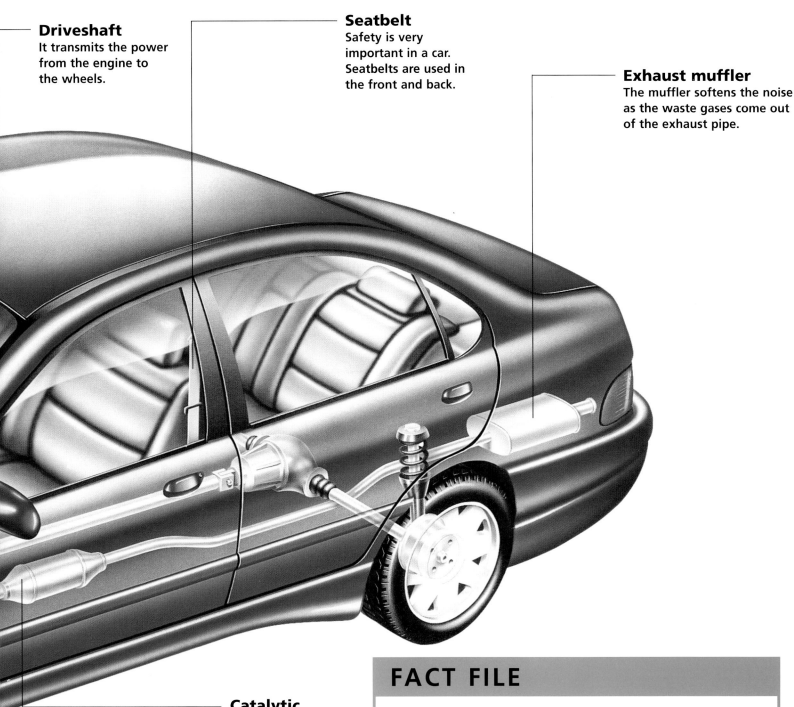

Driveshaft
It transmits the power from the engine to the wheels.

Seatbelt
Safety is very important in a car. Seatbelts are used in the front and back.

Exhaust muffler
The muffler softens the noise as the waste gases come out of the exhaust pipe.

Catalytic converter
Engines give out a lot of poisonous chemicals. With a "cat" fitted, fewer of these chemicals enter the earth's atmosphere.

Gears and drive
Different gears are used to travel at different speeds.

FACT FILE

◯ The largest car ever built is over 60 feet (18m) long. It has a swimming pool in the back.

◯ Andy Green became the first person to travel faster than the speed of sound in a car. In 1997 he drove the Thrust SuperSonic Car at more than 763 miles per hour (1,228km/h) in Nevada.

◯ In 1896 cars were not allowed to travel faster than 12 miles per hour (19km/h).

Engines: under the hood

Most cars are powered by petrol-burning engines, which convert the energy released by burning a mixture of petroleum and air into movement that is used to turn the wheels.

The heart of a car engine is its cylinders. Most have four. The cylinders are where the petrol and air mixture is ignited (set on fire) by spark plugs. Each cylinder is fitted with a piston. As each piston moves down its cylinder, it sucks in the petrol and air mixture through a valve. When the piston reaches the bottom of the cylinder, the valve closes, and the piston starts to move back up again.

The movement of the piston squashes the mixture of petrol and air. Just before the piston reaches the top of the cylinder, the mixture is ignited by a spark plug. The force of the explosion drives the piston back down into the cylinder. Then the piston rises again and forces out any waste gases through another valve. The cycle begins again, with the piston drawing in fresh fuel and air. This type of engine is known as a four-stroke engine.

Cranking the crank

The vertical (up and down) movement of the pistons is turned into rotary (round and round) movement by a part of the engine to which the pistons are attached: it is called the crankshaft. The rotary movement of the crankshaft is transmitted to the wheels that drive the car along. This is just like riding a bicycle, where the vertical movement of your

This diagram shows all the parts of a petrol-powered internal combustion engine.

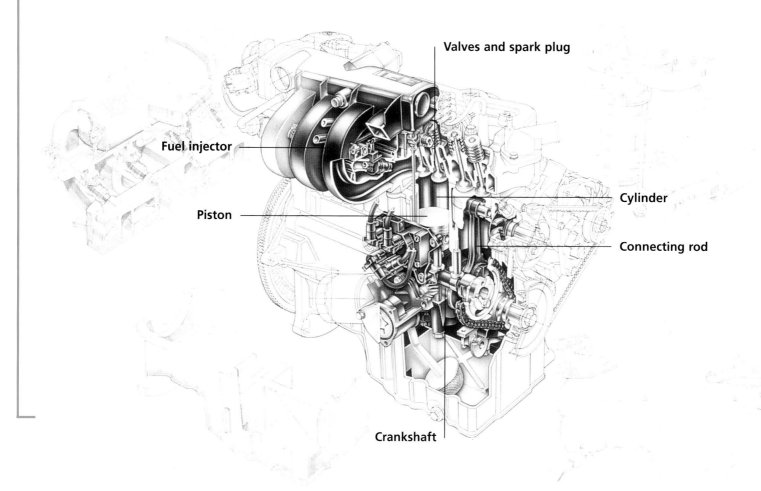

Valves and spark plug

Fuel injector

Piston

Cylinder

Connecting rod

Crankshaft

The engine fits under the car's hood.

feet is turned into rotary movement by the pedals, which is then used to turn the back wheel. The crankshaft also controls the opening and closing of the engine's valves at just the right moment.

The petrol and air that are burned in most cars used to be mixed in a device called a carburettor before being burned in the engine. Modern engines use a gas-injector pump, which is controlled by a computer. This is known as fuel injection.

No spark needed

Diesel engines differ from petrol-burning engines because they do not suck in a mixture of petrol and air. Instead, they draw in air, squash it to the point where it becomes incredibly hot, and then force in diesel oil, which is thicker and burns hotter than petrolium fuel. The oil burns rapidly in the hot air and drives the piston back down into the cylinder. Diesel engines are more efficient than petrol ones and are most commonly used in large vehicles like trucks.

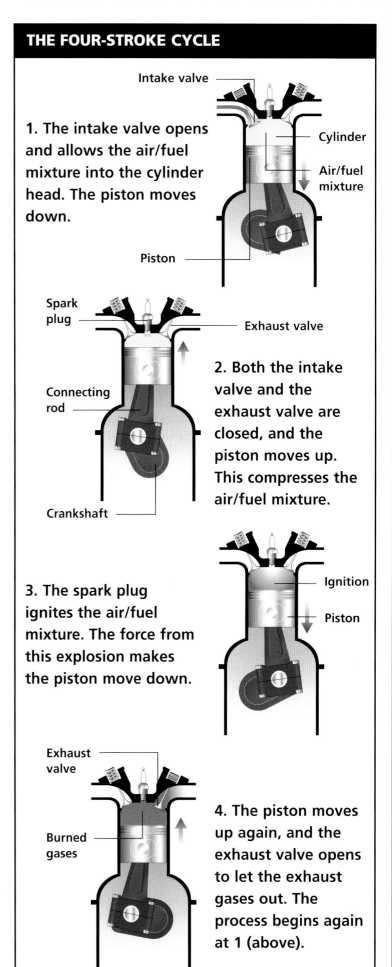

THE FOUR-STROKE CYCLE

1. The intake valve opens and allows the air/fuel mixture into the cylinder head. The piston moves down.

Intake valve

Cylinder

Air/fuel mixture

Piston

Spark plug

Exhaust valve

Connecting rod

Crankshaft

2. Both the intake valve and the exhaust valve are closed, and the piston moves up. This compresses the air/fuel mixture.

Ignition

Piston

3. The spark plug ignites the air/fuel mixture. The force from this explosion makes the piston move down.

Exhaust valve

Burned gases

4. The piston moves up again, and the exhaust valve opens to let the exhaust gases out. The process begins again at 1 (above).

Releasing waste gases

The fuel burned in a car engine turns into gases that have to be released into the air. Some of the gases are poisonous and can damage the environment. Exhaust systems reduce the effects of these gases.

When petrol and air are burned together inside an engine, they produce hot water vapour, carbon dioxide, and a small amount of poisonous gases. Together they are

A blanket of smog (smoke and fog) lies over Los Angeles, California. Most of the smog is caused by car pollution.

CATALYTIC CONVERTER

A catalytic converter changes poisonous exhaust gases into less harmful waste products. The exhaust gases are forced through filters containing the metals platinum and rhodium. These metals cause—and speed up—reactions between the gases. The gases are broken down and then form other, less harmful gases, which are released from the exhaust pipe.

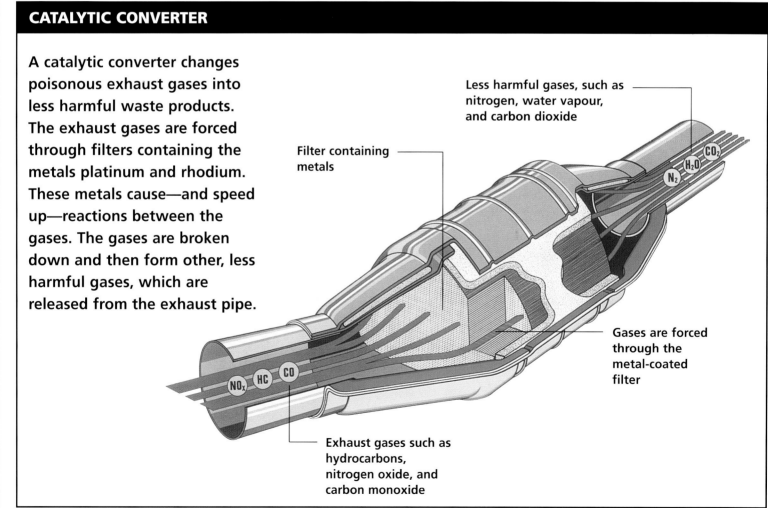

Less harmful gases, such as nitrogen, water vapour, and carbon dioxide

Filter containing metals

Gases are forced through the metal-coated filter

Exhaust gases such as hydrocarbons, nitrogen oxide, and carbon monoxide

known as exhaust gases, and they can pollute the environment and help cause global warming. The waste gases have to be pushed out of the engine's cylinders to allow a fresh supply of petrol and air to be drawn in. If they are not completely removed, the fresh mixture will not ignite properly, and the engine will eventually stop running. The exhaust gases are therefore forced out of the engine cylinders, through an exhaust pipe, and into the open air.

ACID RAIN

○ Acid rain is made when poisonous chemicals are soaked up by water in the atmosphere. The chemicals mostly come from car exhaust pipes and from factories. The water forms droplets of rain, which falls back to earth. When the rain falls, the poisonous chemicals fall with it. This "acid rain" causes damage to crops and trees and even to humans and buildings. It is very difficult to control, because once the chemicals are in the atmosphere, they can travel for hundreds of miles.

Quieter and cleaner

The sound the exhaust gases make as they leave the engine is very loud, and so most cars have a muffler fitted into the exhaust pipe. This device reduces the noise made by the gases by steadily controlling their release, rather than letting them all out at once.

Another device often fitted into the exhaust system is a catalytic converter to reduce the pollution caused by car engines. Many countries have made it against the law to buy a new car that does not have a modern catalytic converter.

Some types of petrol have lead in them. Lead is a type of heavy metal and can cause several illnesses, including brain damage. Cars that use leaded petrol release dangerous lead chemicals into the air through their exhaust. Again, many countries have made it against the law to use leaded fuel.

EFFECTS OF ACID

1 You will need some pieces of eggshell, some vinegar, and a jam jar.

2 Place a piece of eggshell in a jam jar, and add the vinegar to it so it covers the shell. Leave it for a few hours or overnight. What happens to the eggshell?

3 The eggshell contains a chalky material that is corroded by the acid in vinegar. This material in eggshells is also in limestone and marble. Acid rain eats away at stone buildings.

Gears and drive

Cars, like most other vehicles, usually have more than one gear. Different gears are used to transfer power from the engine to the wheels. Lower gears are used for pulling away or going up steep hills. Higher gears are used for travelling along very straight and flat sections of roads.

Cars, like people, find it much easier to travel along a flat road than to climb up a hill. In fact, some of the earliest cars had great difficulty getting up anything steeper than a gentle slope. To get around this problem, engineers fitted a system of gears into the transmission. (The transmission system takes power from the engine to the wheels.) The gears, which are similar to the gears on a bicycle, could be switched

CLUTCH AND GEARBOX

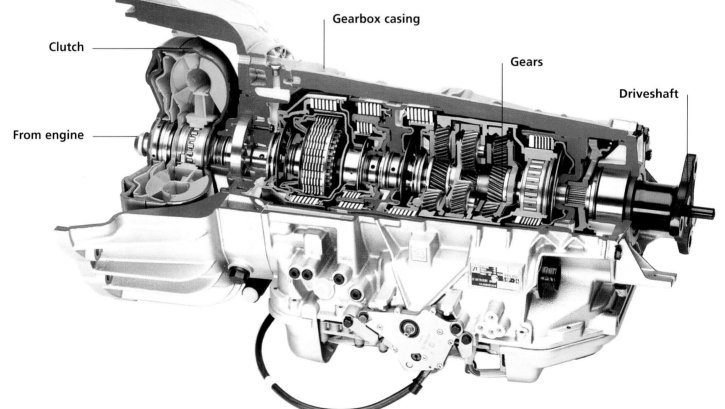

Clutch

From engine

Gearbox casing

Gears

Driveshaft

This cutaway section shows a clutch and gearbox. The clutch is automatic. This means that the driver does not have to press the clutch pedal before changing gears. The car judges when it is the right time to change to another gear by itself.

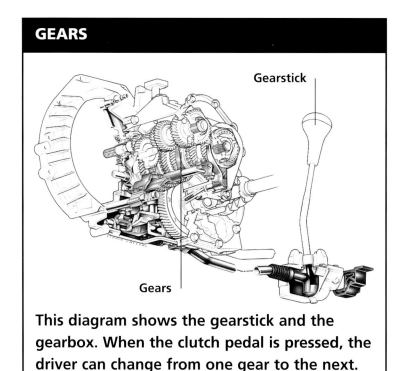

Gearstick

Gears

This diagram shows the gearstick and the gearbox. When the clutch pedal is pressed, the driver can change from one gear to the next.

focused on getting started or getting up the hill. The second gear can also be used to get up steep hills, but only if the car is already moving. Third and fourth gears are used to gain speed once the car is moving fast enough to allow the driver to change up from second gear.

Changing up and down

With the higher gears (third and fourth) the engine's energy is transferred to much larger cogs, which make the drive wheels turn much faster. Changing between the gears can be done by the driver, using the gearstick and the clutch. This temporarily separates the engine from the transmission while the driver chooses a new gear. Some cars are equipped with an automatic gearbox, which changes gears without the driver using a clutch. When the car is turning a corner, a special gear system called a differential allows the wheel on the outside of the turn to travel a much greater distance than the inside wheel (*see* page 15).

depending on the road conditions. First gear is used when pulling away from a standing start or when driving up a really steep hill. Although the engine might be turning very quickly, the drive wheels do not move very fast at all. Instead, all the engine's energy is

ACTION OF GEARS

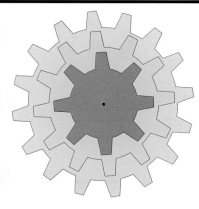

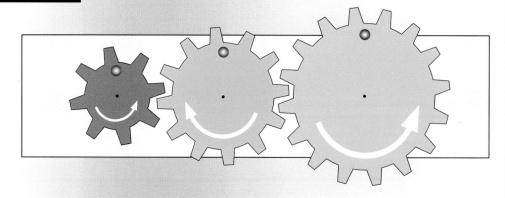

1 Trace the shapes of each of these three gear wheels onto three pieces of cardboard. Cut them out.

2 Pin the wheels to a board in a line from the smallest to the largest. Mark a dot at the top of each one.

3 Count how many times the smaller wheels turn with one turn of the large wheel. This is how car gears work.

Suspension and steering

Cars are fitted with a set of springs and shock absorbers, called the suspension system. It helps keep all four wheels on the road and makes the vehicle safer to drive. Without the suspension we would be badly shaken by every bump or hole on the road, and the car would be almost impossible to control at high speeds.

The main part of the suspension system is a strong, thick spring, which is placed between each wheel hub and the body of the automobile. To stop the car body from bouncing around on the springs, each wheel hub is equipped with a shock absorber. The shock absorbers remove energy from the system to keep the body as steady as possible.

It is easy to see the suspension springs and shock absorbers on this Ford car.

○ When cars were first built, they did not have any suspension. It was added very quickly, because people realised that it was helpful for steering and control as well as comfort.

○ Suspension is now very popular on mountain bikes as well as cars.

○ Take a look for the suspension around the wheels of your car—can you see the shock absorbers and springs? Are they clean or dirty?

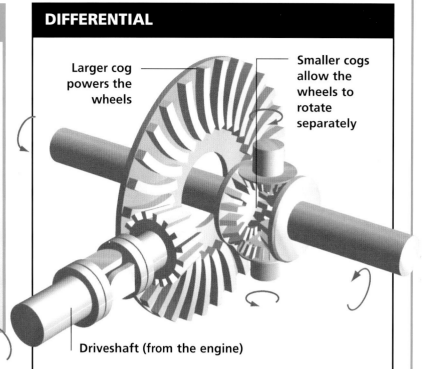

DIFFERENTIAL

Larger cog powers the wheels

Smaller cogs allow the wheels to rotate separately

Driveshaft (from the engine)

The differential allows the left and right wheels to spin at different speeds as the car turns a corner.

Change of direction

The car is steered by the driver, who moves the steering wheel in the direction that the vehicle has to go. The steering wheel is attached to a long shaft, which goes down to a simple gear mechanism. The gear mechanism converts the rotary movement of the steering wheel into side-to-side motion. This is picked up by another shaft that pushes the front wheels of the car to the left or right depending on which way the steering wheel is turned.

As the front wheels go around a bend in the road, they do not stay quite parallel (in a straight line) with each other. This is because the wheel on the inside of the bend has to tilt slightly because it has to make a sharper turn than the outside wheel.

This image shows a power steering mechanism on a car. The steering wheel turns both wheels at the same time. Power steering makes the wheels very easy to turn.

Brakes, wheels and tyres

Most modern cars are equipped with at least one pair of disk brakes. Disk brakes work just like the brakes on a bicycle. A large disk, which looks a little like a solid metal bicycle wheel, is fitted just behind the wheels.

When the driver presses the brake pedal, a pair of brake pads clamps each of the disks, slowing the car down until it eventually stops. Pressure from the driver's foot is transmitted to the brake pads by a special kind of oil, known as brake fluid. It is sealed inside steel tubing and cannot be squashed.

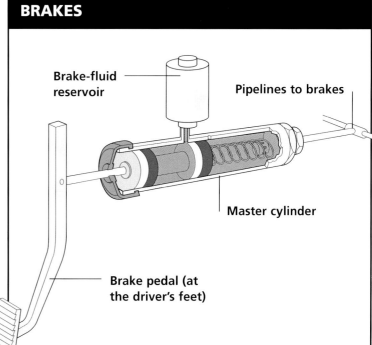

BRAKES

Brake-fluid reservoir

Pipelines to brakes

Master cylinder

Brake pedal (at the driver's feet)

As the driver presses on the brake pedal, the fluid in the cylinder is forced along to the brakes, making them push on the wheels.

This means that when the driver presses on the brake pedal, the pressure is sent in equal amounts to each of the brake pads.

Usually the force in the brakes is amplified (made stronger) with a control system that uses power from the engine. It reduces the amount of strength that the driver personally needs to use to slow down or stop his or her heavy car.

This tyre is filled with air for a smooth ride. There is a pattern on the tread to allow water to be pushed out so that the rubber can grip a wet road surface.

FRICTION SLIDE

1 Place various pieces of different materials on the edge of a wooden or plastic board. Good examples are glass, stone, rubber, and wood. Lift the board up slowly, as in the diagram. Notice how some of the materials have better grip than others.

2 Tyres are needed to grip the road, so which of the materials would be the best to make tires from?

Light but strong

A car rolls along on a set of four wheels. They have to be both lightweight (so that they are less likely to bounce off the road) yet strong enough to take the weight of the vehicle and cope with normal road conditions. Car wheels are nearly always equipped with tyres filled with air, which help make the ride smoother and more comfortable. The tyres

This cutaway diagram shows what is inside an car's wheel. Fluid presses on the brake pads and forces them to tighten on the revolving disk, which is attached to the wheel of the car.

also have a natural or synthetic rubber coating, which is especially thick on the part of the tyre that makes contact with the road. This thick coating stops the tyre from being cut to pieces as it moves along the road surface. Specially shaped grooves are cut into the tyre to help it grip the road. The grooves also help clear any water out of the way as the car is moving along.

Faster and slower

Brakes are not the only way to slow a car. The first way that drivers will stop accelerating (going faster) is by taking their foot off the accelerator pedal. This allows less gas to run into the engine, and the car begins to slow down naturally because of friction and aerodynamics (*see* page 19) and the work required to pull air into the engine past the throttle.

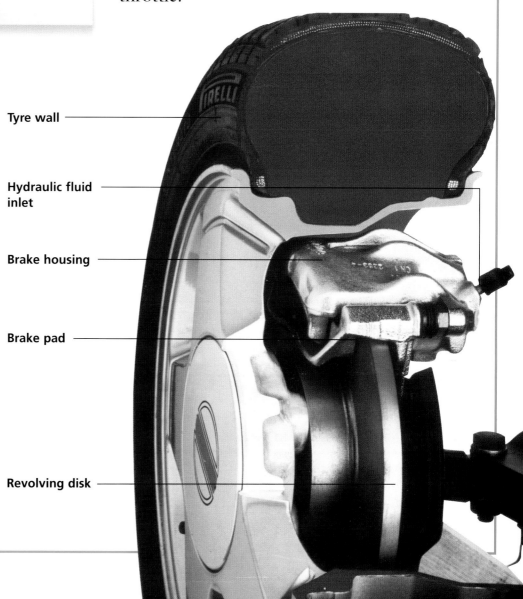

Tyre wall

Hydraulic fluid inlet

Brake housing

Brake pad

Revolving disk

Bodywork–holding it all together

When people first began to build cars, they based their designs on the only thing that was similar at the time, the horse-drawn carriage. Gradually, however, the designs changed and began to look more like the automobiles we are familiar with today.

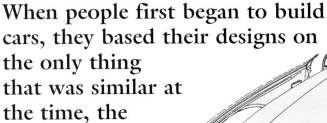

Vehicles like the Ford Model T, while far more practical than earlier designs, were shaped like boxes. This did not present a problem at the time, but as car speeds began to increase, these box-like shapes were found to cause too much drag as the vehicles moved

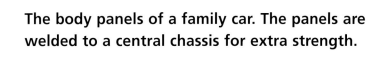

The body panels of a family car. The panels are welded to a central chassis for extra strength.

through the air and actually slowed them down. In order to get around this problem, engineers began to design cars that could cut through the air more easily. These new aerodynamic designs (as they were called) proved to be faster, more stable, and more fuel efficient.

Shaped for use?
Speed, stability, and fuel efficiency are not the only things that influence the way an automobile looks. Often the shape of a vehicle is determined by what it will be used for. The most important thing to consider

This Chevrolet Corvette was built with a plastic body in 1953. The plastic was bolted to a metal chassis. It was the first plastic car to be produced.

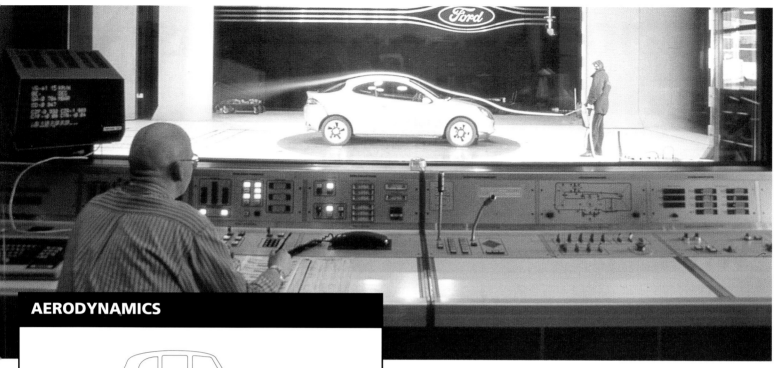

These illustrations show how the shape of cars has changed over the last 100 years. Cars have become closer to the ground and much more streamlined. A lot of this is because of aerodynamic testing.

Above: A car is tested for its ability to cut through the air when on the road. The white line shows the air passing over the car.

when designing a truck, for instance, is just how much storage space can be fitted into the design. Other people require a car that can serve as an ordinary family vehicle most of the time but which is equipped with fold-down seats and a large boot so that big objects can be carried from time to time.

Most car bodies are made from steel that has been pressed into individual panels and then welded to a strong frame. These panels are often slightly curved, like an arch bridge, to give them extra strength.

FACT FILE

○ Cars today do not have a separate chassis. It is attached to the body panels, and this helps strengthen the whole structure.

○ Have you seen any cars made from alternative materials? (Have a look at sports cars and on the Internet.)

19

Interiors and controls–in the driver's seat

Modern cars are not designed just to get us from one place to another. Most drivers, and their passengers, also expect the journey to be a pleasant and comfortable one.

Car designers put a lot of thought into designing the interior of their vehicles. This thinking starts at the floor and carries right on up to the roof. For instance, carpets are usually put into a car but are not there simply to make the interior look nice.

Light switches | Temperature gauge | RPM counter | Speedometer | Fuel gauge | Air inlets | Radio/CD player | Gearstick

Headrest   Folding seat   Armrest   Safety handle   Hand brake   Seat adjusters   Steering wheel

They also make the inside of the car much quieter by absorbing some of the road noise and engine noise.

The seats are specially designed to provide support for the back and the neck. Many of them can be adjusted to fit people of different shapes and sizes. The seats used by the driver and the front passenger can also be moved forward and backward so that adjustments can be made to the amount of legroom to operate pedals correctly and to suit the passengers behind.

Comfort and safety

The most important person in the car is always the driver. For this reason the entire vehicle is usually designed with the driver in mind. All of the controls that the driver needs to use while on the road must be within easy reach. If they were not, the driver would have to take his or her eyes off the road to reach a particular control and so risk having an accident. Any dials, such as the speedometer or the fuel gauge, must also be clearly visible. The driver should only have to glance at them to find out how fast the car is going or how much gas is left in the tank.

FACT FILE

○ Luxury cars have leather interiors, but most car seats are made of plastic or fabric.

○ Can you design an ideal car interior with controls for the whole car? Everything must be easily accessible to the driver.

Off-road and rally cars

Not every car is designed to be used on the road. Some cars, known as off-road vehicles, have been specially adapted to cope with steep hills, mud, and water.

Unlike most normal cars, off-road vehicles are equipped with four-wheel drive. This means that the power from the engine is sent to all four wheels rather than just the back two or the front two. This helps to push and pull the off-road vehicle over all kinds of

tough obstacles. Because there is an increased chance of the vehicle turning over in these conditions, most off-roaders are fitted with a roll cage. It is a strong structure made of tubes of steel that protects the driver of the vehicle from being crushed in case the car should turn over.

Strong on top and below

Off road there is always the danger of the underside of the car being damaged by a collision with rocks or small mounds of earth.

To guard against this, the off-road vehicle sits much higher off the ground than an ordinary car.

Extra wide tyres with very deep tread are also put on the vehicle to improve grip during hill climbs and on muddy stretches. The vehicle also has more low gears to help it cope with these conditions, as well as much tougher suspension to handle all the bumping around.

Normal road cars are sometimes adapted for off-road racing by adding all of the above features. Many of the comfort items are removed, such as carpets, front and rear passenger seats, and sometimes most of the window glass.

This rally car is easily driving through muddy water. It uses four-wheel drive so that power is sent to all of its wheels. The wing, or spoiler, on the back helps the aerodynamics.

Safety–looking after you

The inside of a car is never a safe place to be during a crash, but it is a lot safer than it used to be. Many cars are now equipped with airbags as well as seatbelts to protect the driver in the event of an accident.

Cars can be dangerous. An airbag is an inflatable pillow that is stored in the instrument panel or the steering wheel. During a crash the airbag inflates in an instant and absorbs the force of the driver as he or she is thrown forward by the impact.

Another common safety device is the seatbelt. It is a harness designed to keep the driver and passengers safely in their seats during a crash. The modern seatbelt has a device called an inertia reel. It allows the driver and passengers to move around freely within their seats during a normal journey but locks tight if pulled hard, as would happen during a crash.

Two cars hit each other at 40 miles per hour (64km/h). Don't worry—it was a test, and the cars were being "driven" by crash-test dummies.

Designed to crumple
The bodywork of a car is often designed with special crumple zones, which collapse easily on impact. Crumple zones absorb the energy of a crash before it reaches the driver and passengers. They are usually placed at the front and rear of the vehicle.

Just before they are about to crash, many drivers hit the brakes hard and try to steer out of the way of the object they are about to hit. Unfortunately, this usually makes the

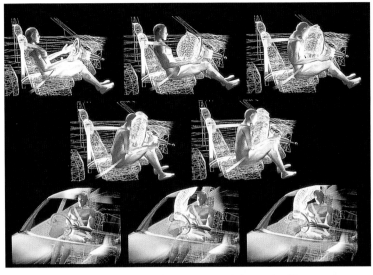

This sequence shows how an airbag inflates to protect the driver of a car. The airbag is usually stored inside the steering wheel or dash.

brakes lock up and the car skid directly in the direction of the object that the driver was trying to avoid. Antilock braking systems (ABS) stop this from happening by automatically releasing the brakes momentarily in the event of a skid, allowing the driver to steer out of trouble and stop safely.

Cars are tested extensively. Manufacturers learn a lot about where they need to strengthen cars by using dummies in artificial crashes.

1978
KPW-11326

RHS

Racing cars–top speed and full power

In many ways the modern racing machine could not be less like a normal car. It has only one seat, terrible fuel economy, and no radio. What it does have is speed and power, and lots of both.

Race cars are built for maximum speed and the best possible road holding. They are specially shaped to cut through the air far more easily than a normal car and are equipped with small wings known as spoilers. They are designed not to get the vehicle into the air but to work in the opposite direction, forcing the race car down hard against the track. To save time during gear changes, and to make the whole operation much smoother, modern race cars have the gear lever built into the steering wheel. Gauges in the cockpit let the driver know how efficiently the vehicle

A Formula One (F1) car. There is a high adhesive rubber on the tyres, making them stick to the road.

is running, and this information is also sent to the support team via a radio link.

Extra grip

The race car has special sticky tyres made of soft synthetic rubber, which grip the track far tighter than normal tyres. Unfortunately, because the tyres are so soft, they wear out very quickly and have to be changed at least once during a race. Tyre changing normally takes place during the pit stop. The race car will stop in a special enclosure, called the pit, which is at the side of the track. While it is stopped, a team of mechanics attempt to change the tyres in record time, put in fuel, fix any minor problems before they develop into major ones, and then send the race car back into the race.

Below: Two drivers crash during a NASCAR race. The cars travel at up to 200mph (320km/h).

SPECIAL STEERING

Gear-
change
paddle

Digital
readout

Warning
light

This is a steering wheel from a Formula One car. The driver changes gear using the "paddles" behind. The readout gives the driver information about the car and its engine.

Cars of the future

In the future the petrol that powers our cars is going to run out. Car manufacturers are already looking for alternative forms of fuel, and there is every chance that the cars of the future will be powered by one of them.

Solar panels, which draw energy directly from the sun and turn it into electricity, were once thought to be the way forward but so far have failed to produce enough energy to power a family-sized vehicle. This means that we are likely to be using batteries to power cars in the future. These batteries will be built into the body of the vehicle and can be recharged overnight.

Above: This is a prototype (test car) that Ford has developed. It is very streamlined, so it will cut through the air easily. It runs on a mixture of petrol and other fuels. It is called the Ford 2010.

Running on gas

Manufacturers are also experimenting with cars that can run on compressed natural gas (CNG), and already there are vehicles on the road that can run on either CNG or diesel. Other alternatives to ordinary petrol include the hydrogen fuel cell, which allows vehicles to run on the energy produced when hydrogen and oxygen combine.

Scientists are also experimenting with vehicles powered by liquid nitrogen. Nitrogen makes up the majority of the earth's atmosphere, so the fuel for these vehicles is likely to be readily available.

Regenerative motors, which draw energy from points in the vehicle's operation where it might normally be wasted, such as during braking, are also proving to be popular with manufacturers of alternative fuel vehicles.

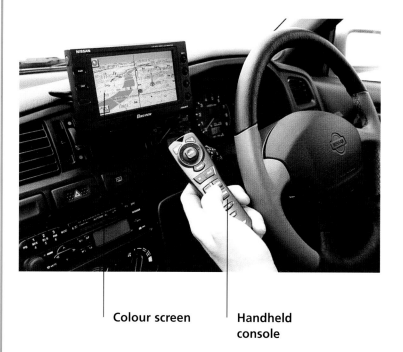

Colour screen | Handheld console

This is a car-mounted navigation system. The driver inputs the destination, and the computer gives him or her full directions.

FACT FILE

◯ Have you seen any "alternative" power cars on the road?

◯ Find some alternative power cars. Start with www.greenculture.com.

Don't get lost

Fewer drivers will be getting lost in the future thanks to the Global Positioning System (GPS). A GPS can be fitted into almost any car. It communicates with satellites in orbit around the earth in order to calculate precisely where the car is and then translates this information to a map display on the dashboard. Alternatively, an on-board computer will interpret this information and tell the driver where to turn off in order to reach the desired destination.

This car runs on battery power. As you can see in the boot, it needs a lot of batteries!

Glossary

AERODYNAMICS—a science dealing with the forces exerted by air on any objects moving through it.

AUTOMATIC—an action that happens without a person requesting it.

CARBURETTOR—a device that allows fuel into the cylinders of an engine.

CATALYTIC CONVERTER—device fitted into exhaust systems to remove harmful substances from the waste gases.

CLUTCH—control that allows the driver to disconnect the engine from the transmission in order to change gear.

CYLINDER—the part of the internal combustion engine in which the fuel is ignited to move the pistons.

DIESEL OIL—fuel-oil petroleum product burned in some cars.

DRAG—the resistance experienced by an automobile as it pushes through air.

EFFICIENT—something that works without too much waste; productive.

FUEL INJECTION—a device that squirts fuel into the cylinders of an engine.

GEAR—toothed wheel that transmits the movement of one shaft to another.

GEARBOX—set of gears designed to make the best use of power from an engine.

HYDRAULICS—a science dealing with practical uses for liquids.

INEFFICIENT—something that works but is wasteful of energy or fuel; unproductive.

INTERNAL COMBUSTION ENGINE— engine that burns fuel inside it.

PETROL—petroleum product used mainly as fuel for cars

PISTON—device used in internal combustion engines to harness power.

PRODUCTION LINE—a factory where goods are put together part by part.

REGENERATIVE MOTOR—a motor that gets power when another energy source is being used, for example, storing braking energy for later use.

SPARK PLUG—electrical component used to provide the spark to ignite the petrol/air mixture in an internal combustion engine.

STREAMLINED—an object that cuts through the air in an efficient manner.

TRANSMISSION—complex arrangement of shafts and gears designed to transmit the power of the engine to the drive wheels.

VALVE—A simple mechanical device that opens and closes to control the flow of a gas or liquid.

FURTHER INFORMATION

Books to read:
The A-to-Z Book of Cars by Angela Royston. Barron's; New York, NY, 1991.
Mighty Machines: Race Car by Caroline Bingham. DK Publishing; New York, NY, 1998.

Web sites to look at:
http://www.japanauto.com
http://www.hfmgv.org
http://abcsn.com/nautomus.htm

Alternatively, try your school or local library.

In 1998 Volkswagen started to sell the "New Beetle"—an updated version of their most popular car. The New Beetle can travel over 700 miles (1,127km) on one tank of fuel.

Index

PICTURE CREDITS Corbis 18bl, 26b Franck Seguin, 27b Kevin Fleming **Daimler Chrysler** 4lc **Mary Evans Picture Library** 4tr **Ford Motor Company** 5t, 8b, 10b, 13tl, 14b, 15bl, 19t, 25tl, 25b, 28 & 29t **Image Bank** 10tr Ulf E. Wallin, 29bl Jeff Smith **Renault UK** 22 & 23b and cover **Rover Group** 9tl and cover, 18tr **TRH Pictures** 3b, 12b, 16bl, 20b and cover, 21t, 24t, 28bl **TRW Aftermarket Operations** 17br **Volkswagen AG** 5br, 30b (t-top b-bottom r-right l-left c-center)